FORMULA ONE RACE CARS

by Janet Piehl

Lerner Publications Company • Minneapolis

To my parents, Ann and Rich

Special thanks to Dan Knutson, Formula One journalist

This book is available in two editions:
Library binding by Lerner Publications Company, a division of Lerner Publishing Group
Soft cover by First Avenue Editions, an imprint of Lerner Publishing Group
241 First Avenue North
Minneapolis, MN 55401 U.S.A.

Website address: www.lernerbooks.com

Library of Congress Cataloging-in-Publication Data

Piehl, Janet.
        Formula One race cars / by Janet Piehl.
            p.   cm. — (Pull ahead books)
        Includes index.
        Summary: Introduces the specialized racing cars known as Formula One, describing various parts and how they help the cars to move quickly around a track, and tells about a Formula One race.
        ISBN: 0–8225–0693–9 (lib. bdg. : alk. paper)
        ISBN: 0–8225–9920–1 (pbk. : alk. paper)
        1. Formula One automobiles—Juvenile literature.
    [1. Formula One automobiles. 2. Automobiles, Racing.
    3. Automobile racing.] I. Title. II. Series.
    TL236.P527 2004
    629.228—dc21   2003009445

Manufactured in the United States of America
1 2 3 4 5 6 – JR – 09 08 07 06 05 04

ZOOM! This car moves fast!

This is a Formula One car. What is a Formula One car?

A Formula One car is a kind of race
car. It is built to be light and to race
very quickly. Who builds a Formula
One car?

A team builds a Formula One car. The team also plans, fixes, and drives Formula One cars.

The team has to follow a set of rules to build the car. The set of rules is called a formula. The formula for these cars is called Formula One.

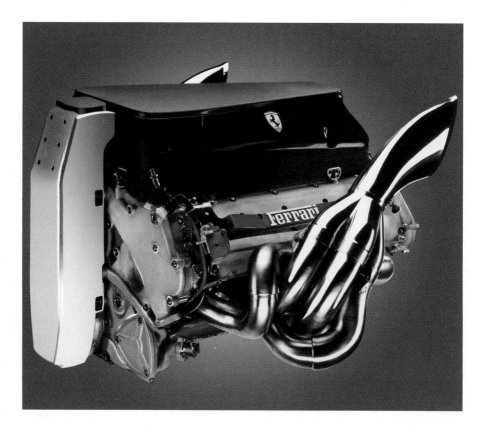

The team puts a powerful **engine** in the car. The engine makes the car go very fast.

The engine sits in back of the car.

The **suspension** connects the wheels to the car.

The **bodywork** covers the engine. It is smooth so the car can zoom down the track.

A Formula One car has **wings.** The wings are on the front and back of the car. Do the wings help the car fly?

No! They keep the car on the ground.
Air moves over the wings and pushes
them down. The wings keep the car
from tipping over.

Today is race day! A Formula One
race is called a **Grand Prix.** The team
gets the car ready to race.

The driver gets into the car. The driver sits in the **cockpit.** Only one person can ride in the cockpit.

The steering wheel and other important controls are in the cockpit.

The cars line up. Off they go! ZOOM!
They start to speed around the track.

The track is curved.

The cars must slow down to go around a curve.

ZOOM! The track is straight. The cars go very fast. Special tires help the car grip the track.

SMASH! Oh no, this car has had an accident! Is the driver hurt?

No. The driver's car protected him. He
wears a helmet and a seatbelt. His
clothes keep him safe from fire.

Why has this car stopped? It needs more gas to make it go. It is going to the **pit.** It needs to make a pit stop.

The team in the pit gives the car more
gas. They also change the car's tires.
ZOOM! The car flies off to finish the race.

The race is almost done. This car passes another. The driver wants to get ahead. Who will win the Grand Prix?

Look! Two cars finish the race. Which one finished first?

This driver and his team have the
fastest car. They win the grand prize!

Facts about Formula One Cars

■ Grand Prix races are about 190 miles long. That is the distance between New York City, New York, and Baltimore, Maryland. The races must stop after two hours.

■ Formula One cars drive at about 200 miles per hour during races. Regular cars drive about 55 miles per hour on the highway.

■ Twenty cars race in a Grand Prix.

■ Drivers want to make pit stops as fast as possible. Some pit stops are only 5 seconds long!

Parts of a Formula One Car

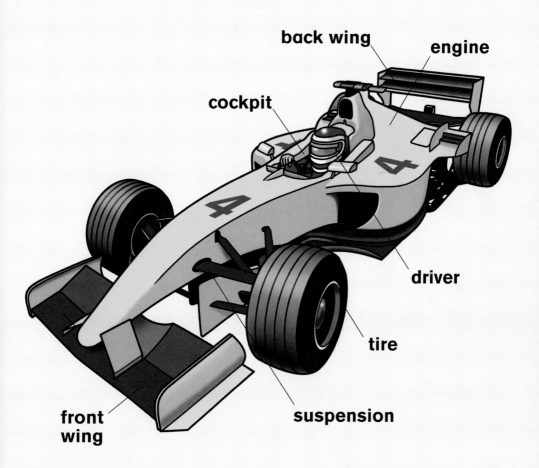

back wing

engine

cockpit

driver

tire

front wing

suspension

Glossary

bodywork: the smooth part of a Formula One car that covers the car's engine

cockpit: the place where the driver sits in a Formula One car

engine: the part that gives the car power to move

Grand Prix: French for "Grand Prize." Grand Prix is the name for a Formula One race.

pit: an area next to the track where a driver can stop to get gas, change tires, and make repairs

suspension: the part of a Formula One car that connects the wheels to the main part of the car

wings: parts on the front and back of a Formula One car that keep the car from tipping over

Index

About the Author

Janet Piehl grew up near Milwaukee, Wisconsin, where she learned to drive slowly. While living in France, she learned to like fast driving and auto racing. She currently lives in Minneapolis, Minnesota, where she rides the bus to work.

Photo Acknowledgments

The photographs in this book are reproduced with permission of: © Bongarts/SportsChrome, pp. 9, 11, 12, 13, 16, 19, 20, 31; © Formula One/1™/Artemis Images, pp. 3, 4, 5, 6, 10, 14, 15, 18, 23, 25, 26, 27; © AFP/CORBIS, pp. 7, 21, 22; © Getty Images, pp. 8, 24; © Mark Thompson/Getty Images, p. 17.

Cover: © Bongarts/SportsChrome.